Book & Article Reviews Log For Therapists & Counsellors

List And Review Your Reading And Apply It To Your Client Work

By Wise Mind Planners

Wise Mind Planners are produced by a practising psychotherapist and writer.

Other publications in this series for therapists and counsellors by Wise Mind Planners:

- *Training & Continuing Professional Development (CPD) Log Book For Therapists & Counsellors: List All Your CPD Courses & Hours In One Place*
- *Appointment Planner 2019 For Therapists & Counsellors (UK edition)*
- *Appointment Planner 2019 For Therapists & Counselors (US edition)*
- *Notepad & Planner For Therapists & Counsellors, Large Lined Pad, 150 Pages*
- *Trainee Counsellors & Therapists Client Hours Logbook: Daily Record Of Completed Client Hours*
- *Notebook For Therapists & Counselors: For Session Notes, Supervision Themes And More (US edition)*
- *Notebook For Therapists & Counsellors: For Session Notes, Supervision Themes And More (UK edition)*
- *Reflections On Personal Therapy For Trainee Counsellors & Therapists: A 50-page Guided Journal*
- *Appointment Planner 2019 For Hypnotherapists*

Cover photo: Angelo Pantazis

This reviews log book belongs to:

Book & Article Reviews Log
For Therapists & Counsellors

List And Review Your Reading And
Apply It To Your Client Work

Whether you're in training or fully qualified, all therapists and counsellors read books, papers and journals as part of their work. Reading widely helps practitioners keep their knowledge up-to-date in this fast-changing field.

This journal allows you to gather all your reading in one place, making it easy to refer back to and apply to your client and written work.

In it you can list:
- Each work's title, author and year of publication
- The approach or school of therapy, eg Psychodynamic
- Memorable quotes and themes
- For each work there is a whole page for you to write about how you'd apply the themes to client work, followed by a page for notes
- Finally, there is a rating scale for how you found the book overall.

There is room for 40 publications, and an index at the front for you to fill in with the titles of your reviews as you go, along with their page number.

Using this log book will allow you to deepen your practice as you reflect on your reading in detail.

Index

Title	Page no
Title	Page no

Index

Title	Page no
Title	Page no

Index

Title	Page no
Title	Page no

Index

Title	Page no

Title	Page no

Book/publication title: ____

____

Author: ____

Approach: ____

Year: __________________________

Memorable quotes & themes	Page no

How I could apply this to client work

Notes

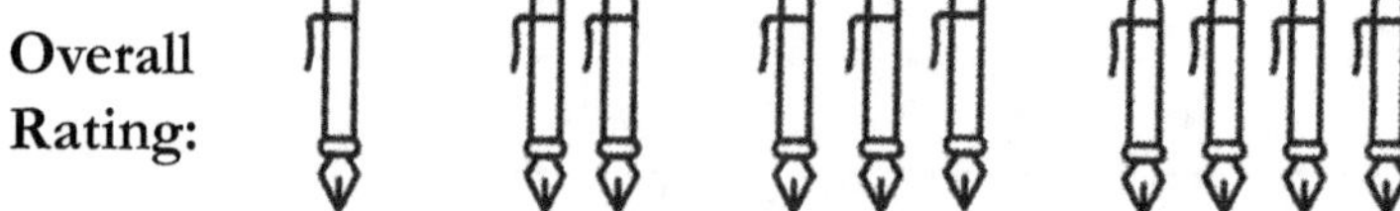

**Overall
Rating:**

Book/publication title: ___________________________________

____

Author: ____

Approach: ____

Year: _______________________________

Memorable quotes & themes	Page no

How I could apply this to client work

Notes

Overall Rating:

Book/publication title: _______________________________

____

Author: ____

Approach: ____

Year: _______________________________

Memorable quotes & themes	Page no

How I could apply this to client work

Notes

Overall
Rating:

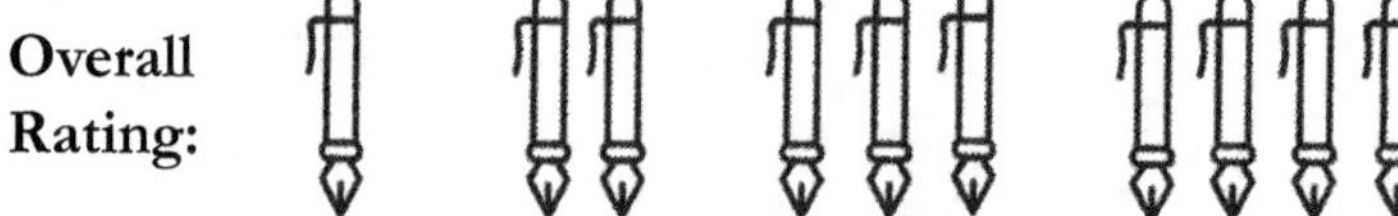

Book/publication title: _______________________________

____

Author: _______________________________

Approach: _______________________________

Year: _______________________________

Memorable quotes & themes	Page no

How I could apply this to client work

Notes

Overall
Rating:    

Book/publication title: ___________________________________

____

Author: ___________________________________

Approach: ___________________________________

Year: ___________________________________

Memorable quotes & themes	Page no

How I could apply this to client work

Notes

Notes

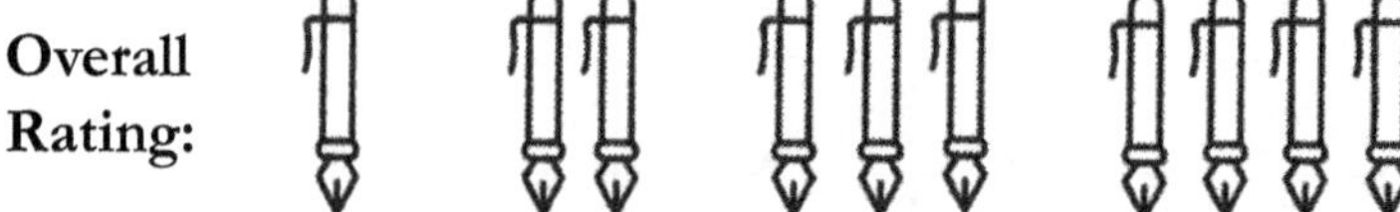

Overall Rating:

Book/publication title: ____

____

Author: ____

Approach: ____

Year: ___________________________

Memorable quotes & themes	Page no

How I could apply this to client work

Notes

Overall Rating:

Book/publication title: __________________________________

____

Author: ____

Approach: ____

Year: ____________________________

Memorable quotes & themes	Page no

How I could apply this to client work

Notes

Overall Rating:

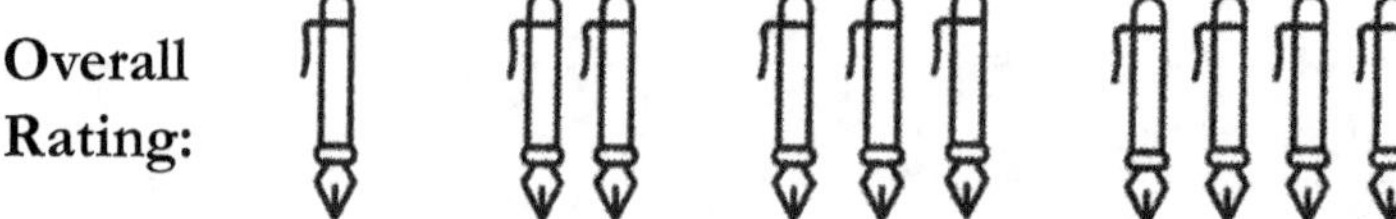

Book/publication title: _______________________________

____

Author: ____

Approach: ____

Year: _______________________

Memorable quotes & themes	Page no

How I could apply this to client work

Notes

Book/publication title: _______________________________________

____

Author: _______________________________________

Approach: _______________________________________

Year: _______________________________

Memorable quotes & themes	Page no

How I could apply this to client work

Notes

Overall Rating:

Book/publication title: ___________________________

____

Author: ____

Approach: _______________________________________

Year: _______________________________

Memorable quotes & themes	Page no

How I could apply this to client work

Notes

Overall
Rating:    

Book/publication title: _______________________________________

____

Author: ____

Approach: ____

Year: _______________________________

Memorable quotes & themes	Page no

How I could apply this to client work

Notes

Overall
Rating:

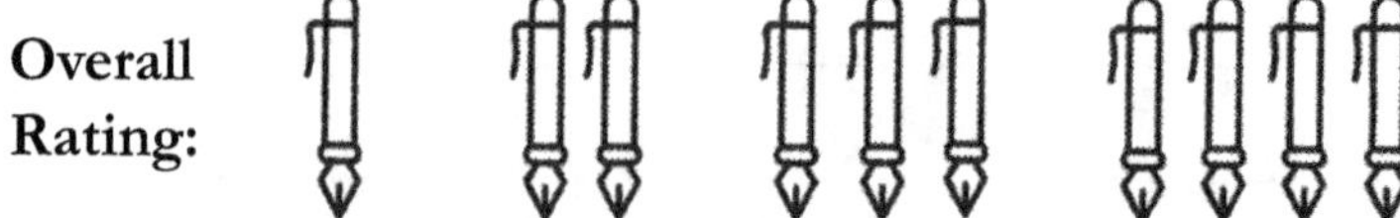

Book/publication title: _______________________________________

____

Author: _______________________________________

Approach: _______________________________________

Year: _______________________________________

Memorable quotes & themes	Page no

How I could apply this to client work

Notes

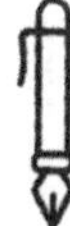

Overall Rating:

Book/publication title: ___________________________

____

Author: ____

Approach: _______________________________________

Year: ___________________________

Memorable quotes & themes	Page no

How I could apply this to client work

Notes

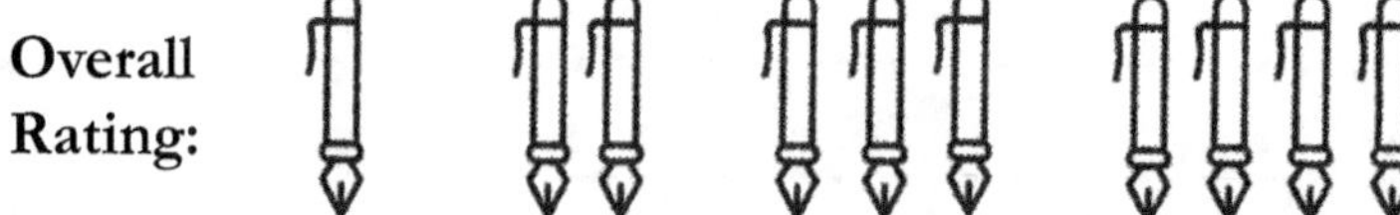

Notes

Overall Rating:

Book/publication title: _______________________________

____

Author: _______________________________________

Approach: _____________________________________

Year: _________________________

Memorable quotes & themes	Page no

How I could apply this to client work

Notes

Overall
Rating:

Book/publication title: _______________________________

____

Author: ____

Approach: ____

Year: _________________________________

Memorable quotes & themes	Page no

How I could apply this to client work

Notes

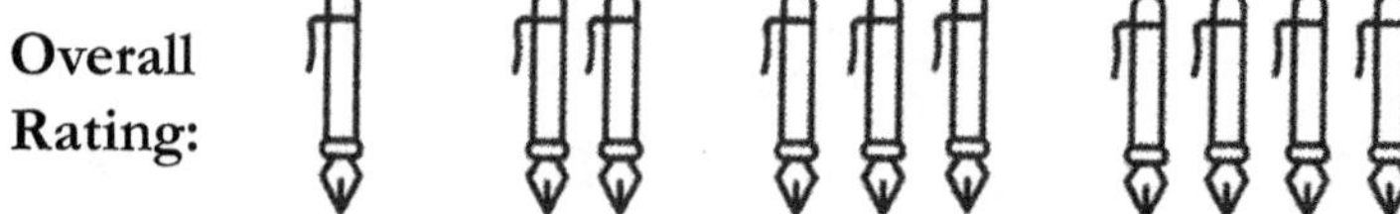

Notes

Overall Rating:

Book/publication title: _______________________________________

____

Author: _______________________________________

Approach: _______________________________________

Year: _______________________

Memorable quotes & themes	Page no

How I could apply this to client work

Notes

Overall
Rating:    

Book/publication title: ___________________________________

____

Author: ___________________________________

Approach: ___________________________________

Year: ___________________________________

Memorable quotes & themes	Page no

How I could apply this to client work

Notes

Overall Rating:

Book/publication title: __________________________________

____

Author: __________________________________

Approach: __________________________________

Year: __________________________________

Memorable quotes & themes	Page no

How I could apply this to client work

Notes

Overall
Rating:   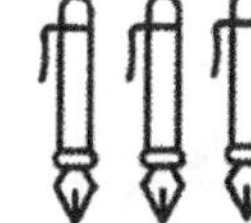 

Book/publication title: _______________________________________

____

Author: _______________________________________

Approach: _______________________________________

Year: _______________________

Memorable quotes & themes	Page no

How I could apply this to client work

Notes

Notes

**Overall
Rating:**

Book/publication title: _______________________________

____

Author: ____

Approach: ____

Year: __________________________

Memorable quotes & themes	Page no

How I could apply this to client work

Notes

Overall Rating:

Book/publication title: ______________________________

____

Author: ______________________________________

Approach: ____________________________________

Year: ______________________

Memorable quotes & themes	Page no

How I could apply this to client work

Notes

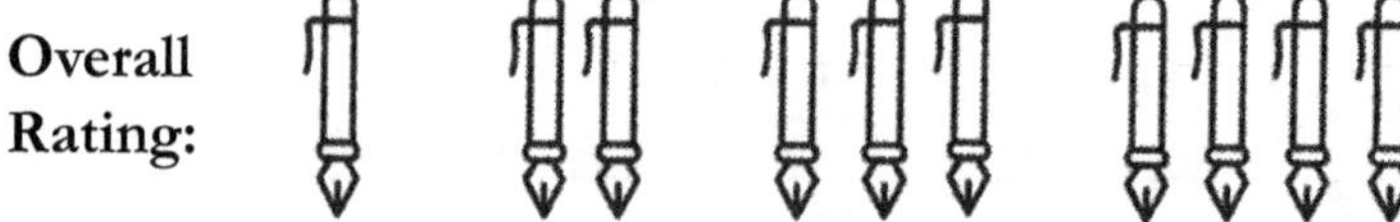

Overall Rating:

Book/publication title: ____

____

Author: ____

Approach: ____

Year: ________________________________

Memorable quotes & themes	Page no

How I could apply this to client work

Notes

Overall
Rating:    

Book/publication title: _______________________________

____

Author: _______________________________

Approach: _______________________________

Year: _______________________________

Memorable quotes & themes	Page no

How I could apply this to client work

Notes

Overall Rating:

Book/publication title: __________________________________

____

Author: __________________________________

Approach: __________________________________

Year: __________________________________

Memorable quotes & themes	Page no

How I could apply this to client work

Notes

Overall Rating:

Book/publication title: __________________________________

____

Author: ____

Approach: ____

Year: ___________________________

Memorable quotes & themes	Page no

How I could apply this to client work

Notes

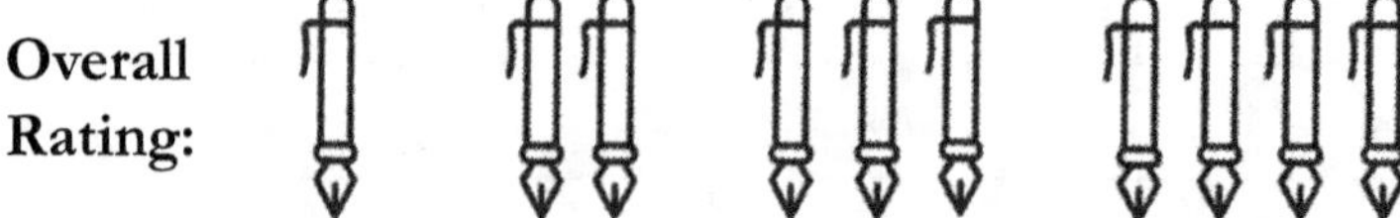

Overall Rating:

Book/publication title: ____

____

Author: ____

Approach: ____

Year: ________________________________

Memorable quotes & themes	Page no

How I could apply this to client work

Notes

Overall
Rating:    

Book/publication title: ______________________________________

____

Author: ______________________________________

Approach: ______________________________________

Year: ______________________________

Memorable quotes & themes	Page no

How I could apply this to client work

Notes

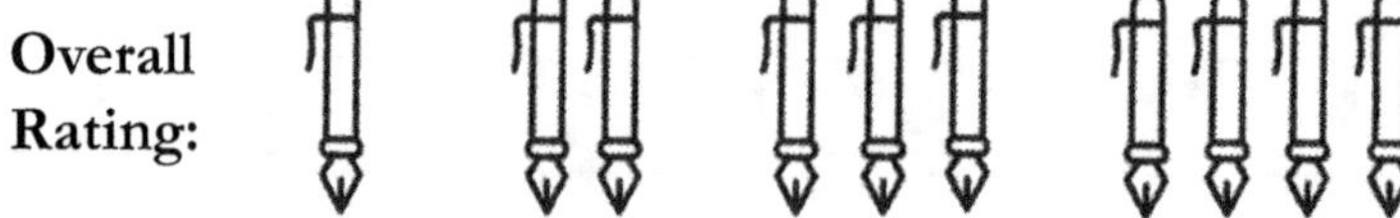

Overall Rating:

Book/publication title: _______________________________

____

Author: ____

Approach: ____

Year: _______________________

Memorable quotes & themes	Page no

How I could apply this to client work

Notes

Overall
Rating:  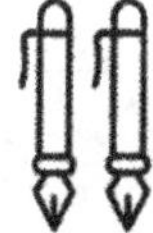  

Book/publication title: ____

____

Author: ____

Approach: ____

Year: ______________________________

Memorable quotes & themes	Page no

How I could apply this to client work

Notes

Overall
Rating:

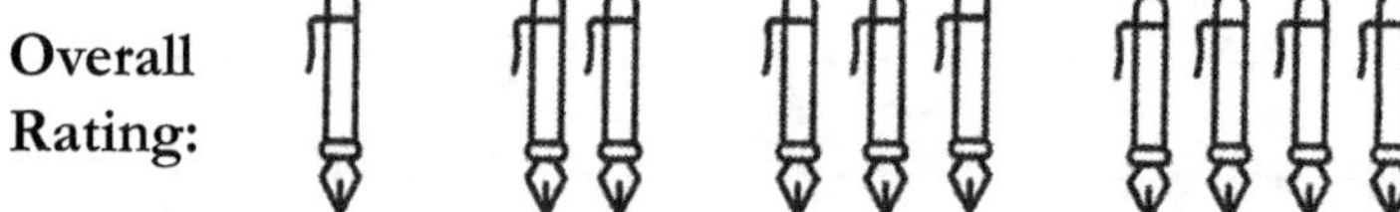

Book/publication title: _______________________________

____

Author: ____

Approach: ____

Year: _______________________________

Memorable quotes & themes	Page no

How I could apply this to client work

Notes

Overall Rating:

Book/publication title: ____

____

Author: ____

Approach: ____

Year: _______________________________

Memorable quotes & themes	Page no

How I could apply this to client work

Notes

Overall Rating:

Book/publication title: _______________________________

____

Author: ____

Approach: ____

Year: _________________________

Memorable quotes & themes	Page no

How I could apply this to client work

Notes

Overall Rating:

Book/publication title: _______________________________

____

Author: _______________________________________

Approach: _____________________________________

Year: _______________________

Memorable quotes & themes	Page no

How I could apply this to client work

Notes

Notes

Overall Rating: 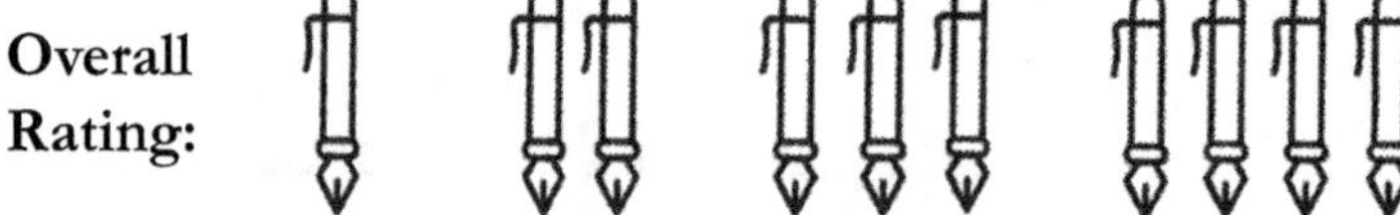

Book/publication title: ___________________________

____

Author: ____

Approach: ____

Year: ______________________________

Memorable quotes & themes	Page no

How I could apply this to client work

**Overall
Rating:**

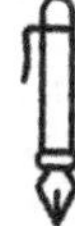

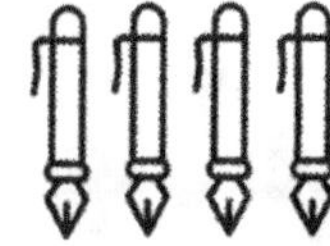

Book/publication title: _______________________________________

____

Author: ____

Approach: ____

Year: _______________________

Memorable quotes & themes	Page no

How I could apply this to client work

Notes

Overall Rating:

Book/publication title: _______________________________

____

Author: _______________________________

Approach: _______________________________

Year: _______________________________

Memorable quotes & themes	Page no

How I could apply this to client work

Notes

Overall Rating:

Book/publication title: _______________________________________

____

Author: ____

Approach: ____

Year: ____________________________

Memorable quotes & themes	Page no

How I could apply this to client work

Notes

Overall
Rating:

Book/publication title: _______________________________

____

Author: ____

Approach: ____

Year: _____________________________

Memorable quotes & themes	Page no

How I could apply this to client work

Notes

Overall Rating:

Book/publication title: ____

____

Author: ____

Approach: ____

Year: ___________________________

Memorable quotes & themes	Page no

How I could apply this to client work

Notes

Overall Rating:

| Book/publication title: _______________________________ |
| ____ |
| Author: ____ |
| Approach: ____ |
| Year: __________________________ |

Memorable quotes & themes	Page no

How I could apply this to client work

Notes

Overall Rating: